From Nazareth to Patmos

OTHER BOOKS BY FRANK VIOLA

Volume 1: Rethinking the Wineskin:
The Practice of the New Testament Church

Volume 2: Who is Your Covering?:
A Fresh Look at Leadership, Authority, and Accountability

Volume 3: Pagan Christianity:
The Origins of Our Modern Church Practices

Volume 4: So You Want to Start a House Church?:
First-Century Styled Church Planting for Today

Knowing Christ Together

The Untold Story of the New Testament Church

Straight Talk to Elders

Visit the Present Testimony Ministry Web Site for
Ordering Information:

www.ptmin.org

FROM NAZARETH TO PATMOS

Frank Viola

To my dear friend and fellow-soldier
in the Kingdom of God . . .
Frank Valdez

CONTENTS

FOREWORD

All over the world Christians are re-exploring the nature and practice of church life. The past 40 years have demonstrated that world-wide, the fastest growing segments of the Christian community are those that are open to the life of Christ as expressed through simpler expressions of church life, usually known as house churches.

So what is this life? For Frank, the explanation is simple and straightforward. It is Christ Himself. He is our life, and He is the life of the church. To understand the Lordship of Christ is to understand the basic ecclesiology and leadership design that God provided for the church. Jesus is the Head of the church, not just in name, but in actuality.

As Tozer noted, "For the true Christian, the supreme test for the present soundness and ultimate worth of everything religious must be the place our Lord occupies in it. Is He Lord or symbol? Is He in charge of the project or merely one of the crew? . . . All religious activities may be proved by the answer to the question: Is Jesus Christ Lord in this act?"[1]

---

[1] A.W. Tozer, *The Waning Authority of Christ in the Churches.*

The natural consequence of this understanding of the leadership of Jesus within the church is to then understand, as Frank puts it later in this book, "The church is simply this: *A community of people who possess the life of God's Kingdom and who express it together.*" Kingdom is foundational to ecclesiology. "The kingdoms of this world are become the kingdoms of our Lord, and of His Christ; and He shall reign for ever and ever."[2] The story of the New Testament is the story of how this is lived out. It is a story of God-inspired consequences. The story of what happens when people live the life of Christ together, without imposing human authority over and above Christ's authority.

The strength of this book is its simplicity and clarity. Frank has a message to share, and it is that Jesus is enough. He does not need man leading His church for Him.

Although this book covers wide ground, it does not cover every aspect of church life. Abraham Lincoln is quoted as saying, "You don't make the weak strong by making the strong weak." And neither do you strengthen this book by trying to point out any areas not emphasized.

Frank has a specific message to share in this book concerning the Kingdom of God as it plays out in the New Testament saga. That is its scope. And we need to hear that message.

Dr. Tony Dale
Austin, Texas

---

[2] Rev. 11:15, KJV.

PREFACE

This book completes my series on radical church reform. In the first volume, *Rethinking the Wineskin*, I compared and contrasted the major practices of the first-century church with those of the modern church.

The second volume, *Who is Your Covering?*, explored the subjects of leadership and authority as they were understood by the early Christians. In the third volume, *Pagan Christianity*, I traced the origin of the modern institutional church and explained why it should be abandoned today. Volume four, *So You Want to Start a House Church?*, treated the various ways that churches were planted in the New Testament (NT) and urged that we return to them today.

Following in the same spirit, *From Nazareth to Patmos* is a narrative ecclesiology[3] that traces the growth and development of the early church. It pays special attention to the theme of the Kingdom of God from Nazareth—with Jesus and the Twelve—to Patmos, the island where John wrote Revelation. The book also lays stress on how far afield the modern church has strayed from its primitive beginnings.

Those desiring a more detailed account of the first-century church should consult my book *The Untold Story of the New Testament Church*. *The Untold Story* is a comprehensive, socio-historical unfolding of the early church in chronological order. It is also a user-friendly NT handbook.

---

[3] Ecclesiology is the theological term for the study of church life and practice.

Finally, I would like to thank the following people for their positive influence on this book: Gene Edwards, Howard Snyder, Hal Miller, Frank Valdez, George E. Ladd, W. Graham Scroggie, and G. Campbell Morgan. Thanks also to Mike Biggerstaff for his superb proofing work.

My hope is that this book, along with the others in this series, will help ignite a full-scale revolution in the Body of Christ. A revolution not bred of men, but of God Himself. A revolution that will restore those intangible elements that marked the lives of the first Christians.

Frank Viola
Jacksonville, Florida
November 2004

The Story is a tale as large as the universe and yet as small as an individual human being. It is, however, not a Story about everything, not even about all of human history. It is a Story that focuses on God's relationship to mankind, from the beginning of the human race in Adam to its climax in the eschatological Adam, and beyond. It is a Story about creation and creature and their redemption by, in, and through Jesus Christ. It is a Story about a community of faith created out of the midst of fallen humanity. It involves both tragedy and triumph, both the lost and the saved, both the first and the last. Its focus is repeatedly on Divine and human actions on the stage of human history. It is out of this Story, which Paul sees as involving both history and His story (i.e., Christ's), that he argues, urges, encourages, debates, promises, and threatens . . . Christ is the central and most crucial character in the human drama, and everything that Paul says about all other aspects of the Story is colored and affected by this conviction . . . In Paul's view, one is always in danger of saying too little about Jesus Christ, not too much.[4]

*   -Ben Witherington*

---

[4] *Paul's Narrative Thought World: The Tapestry of Tragedy and Triumph* (Louisville: Westminster/John Knox Press, 1994), pp. 2-3.

Your Kingdom come, Your will be done on earth as it is in heaven.
-Matthew 6:10

INTRODUCTION

The NT contains a saga. That saga is the unfolding drama of God's ultimate intention. And that intention is centered on the Kingdom of God coming to earth.[5] The Kingdom of God is nothing other than the rule of God. And it rests on the Lordship of Jesus Christ.

The Kingdom of God produces the church. The church, in turn, submits to the sway or rule of the Kingdom. As it does, the church expresses, represents, and advances God's Kingdom on the earth.

Properly conceived, the church is the community of believers who joyfully enthrone Jesus Christ, express His sovereign rule in the world, and as a result, enjoy the blessings of the future age here-and-now.

According to the NT, the church is not a building. Neither is it a denomination, a religious service, nor a non-denominational organization. The church is simply this: *A*

---

[5] The terms "Kingdom of God," "Kingdom of heaven," and "Kingdom of Christ" are used interchangeably throughout the NT. Matthew used the term "Kingdom of heaven," while Mark and Luke used "Kingdom of God." "Heaven" was frequently used by Jews as a reverential way of avoiding the use of the name of God. Matthew wrote to Jews. According to E. Stanley Jones, the Kingdom of God was "the center and circumference of all that He [Jesus] taught and did . . . the Kingdom of God is the master-conception, the master-plan, the master-purpose, the master-will that gathers everything up into itself and gives it redemption, coherence, purpose, goal" (*Is the Kingdom of God Realism?*, New York: Abingdon-Cokesbury, 1940, p. 53).

community of people who possess the life of God's Kingdom and who express it together.

Your NT contains the epic saga of the early church. That saga centers on how God the Father has made Jesus of Nazareth both Lord and King of the universe.

According to the Gospels, the master thought of Jesus was the Kingdom of God which is "at hand."[6] The book of Acts continues this thought and tells the story of how the Kingdom made its introduction in Jerusalem and spread to Rome.[7]

The Kingdom of God is a dual reality. It is "already," but it is "not yet." The Kingdom is present.[8] At the same time, it is future.[9] The Kingdom is today; but it is also tomorrow.

In effect, the future age of the Kingdom is present on the earth even though it is a future reality. With the coming of Christ, the Kingdom that belongs to the future age has broken into this present age. Consequently, as Christians, we are living in the presence of the future.

The Kingdom of God is also a mystery.[10] It does not set out to destroy human authority in this age.[11] Instead, the Kingdom destroys the powers and principalities in the spiritual realm. Its enemy is the kingdom of darkness and the

---

[6] Jesus spoke of the Kingdom over 100 times in the Gospels. The theme appears in Jesus' first message (Mark 1:15) as well as in His last (Acts 1:6).

[7] The book of Acts begins and ends with the Kingdom (Acts 1:1-3; 28:23, 31).

[8] Matt. 11:11-12; 12:28; 21:31; 23:13; Mark 10:15; Luke 16:16; 17:20-21; John 3:3; Rom. 14:17.

[9] Matt. 7:21; 8:11-12; 13:41-43; Mark 10:23; 14:24-25; Luke 12:32; 1 Cor. 15:50; 2 Pet. 1:11; Rev. 11:15.

[10] Matt. 13:11; Mark 4:11; Luke 8:10.

[11] John 18:36.

ruler of this age (Satan). Put another way, the Kingdom of God does not seek to change the political order of things. It rather makes changes in the spiritual order that affect the lives of men and women.[12] The Kingdom works quietly and secretly among men and women. It is not a forceful power that cannot be resisted. The Kingdom is rather like a man planting a seed. Its success depends on the type of soil in which it is planted. Like a mustard seed, its growth is slow and imperceptible. Yet at a future day, the Kingdom will be manifested in great power and glory. The fact that the Kingdom is fulfilled today, yet it is waiting to be consummated, is indeed a mystery.

In all of Paul's letters, the theme of the Kingdom of God appears. However, Paul's letters were primarily written to Gentile audiences. Thus he speaks more of the Lordship of Christ than he does of the Kingdom of God.[13] For Paul, Jesus as Lord is a synonym for the Kingdom. In addition, terms such as "reigning," "rule," "majesty," "Lord Jesus Christ," "King of kings," "Lord of lords," "Christ the Head," "the age to come" all speak of the Kingdom.

Tragically, the saga of the early church has been obscured for centuries because our NT books are arranged out of order.[14] The present arrangement of the NT books has created a seedbed for the very damaging "cut-and-paste" approach to

---

[12] Sometimes the citizens of the Kingdom show its transforming impact, like the Puritans and Abolitionists, by challenging the unjust and ungodly institutions of this age.

[13] The Jews understood the concept of the Kingdom of God because it was prophesied in the Old Testament. It was a fairly new idea for the Gentiles, though they well understood the concepts of lordship and authority.

[14] For a detailed discussion of this topic, see *Pagan Christianity*, Chapter 11.

Bible study, where out-of-context "proof-texts" are lashed together to support man-made doctrines and practices.

In Greek mythology, a man named Procrustes owned a magical bed that had the unique property of matching whoever laid upon it. But his bed was not so magical. Procrustes had a crude method for creating his "one-size-fits-all" bed. If the person laying upon it was too small, Procrustes would stretch his limbs out to fit the bed! If the person was too large, Procrustes would chop off the person's limbs to make them fit!

The modern concept of "church" is a Procrustean bed. Scriptures that do not fit its shape are either chopped off (dismissed) or they are stretched out to fit its mold.

This book turns that bed upside down and begins with an entirely new premise. That premise is that we will never return to a right practice of the church as God ordained it until we first learn the saga of the first-century church. This book narrates the saga in chronological order—beginning at Nazareth, where the seeds of the church were planted—and ending at Patmos, where the saga closes.

As you read through this saga, you will be amazed to discover what is *not* present. Namely, virtually everything that characterizes the modern church today.

That statement is shocking. Nonetheless, it is true. The following are wholly absent from the saga: Church buildings, the Sunday morning order of worship, the weekly sermon, the modern pastoral office, the choir, Sunday school, seminary, Bible college, the clergy, the laity, the clergy costume, the practice of dressing up for church, tithing, pews, pulpits, steeples, and a host of other things that are commonly accepted as Christian practices.[15]

All of these things are contrary to the Kingdom of God. But worst of all, they actually hinder the Kingdom from advancing. That is, they do not reflect the rule of Jesus Christ, nor do they express His Headship over His people. Instead, they reflect the enthronement of man's ideas and traditions.

On the flip side, the saga will enable you to discover how the early church lived by the life of the Kingdom of God and expressed it in the earth. Since Adam's fall, the earth has been under the rulership of Satan, the usurper.[16] Jesus Christ came as the last Adam, to take back the earth and put it under His sovereign rule.[17]

The early church understood this principle, and as a result, made Christ both Lord and Head, giving Him the place of rulership and supremacy. As the church enthrones Jesus Christ, the Kingdom of God spreads throughout the earth. This is precisely what God is after today: *The establishment of His Kingdom on this planet.*

With that said, let us go to a small town called Nazareth, where a certain Carpenter is making preparations to fulfill His greatest desire . . . the bursting forth of His Father's unseen Kingdom into the visible realm.

---

[15] See my book *Pagan Christianity* for a comprehensive discussion on where we got these modern church practices.

[16] Matt. 4:8-9; John 12:31; 14:30; 16:11; 2 Cor. 4:4; Eph. 2:2; 1 John 5:19.

[17] Gen. 1:26-28; Heb. 2:14; 1 Cor. 15:45.

The Kingdom of God is not coming with signs to be observed; nor will they say, "Look, here it is!" or "There it is!" For behold, the Kingdom of God is in your midst."

-Luke 17:20-21

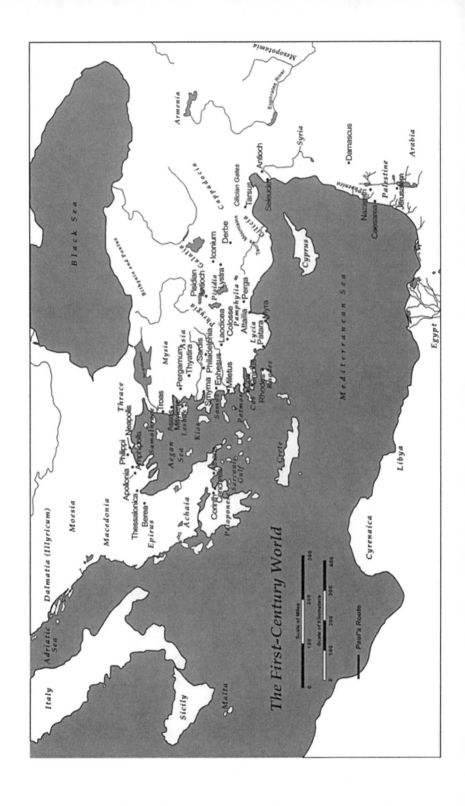

The First-Century World

Scale of Miles
0   100   200   300

Scale of Kilometers
0   100   200   300   400

———— Paul's Route

CHAPTER 1

THE KINGDOM COMES TO NAZARETH
B.C. 4 - A.D. 30

In Bethlehem of Judea, a King is born. This King is the Son of the Most High God. He is Divinity resident in humanity and is given the name *Jesus.*

Jesus grows up in the ill-reputed town of Nazareth, plying His trade in a carpenter's shop. God the Father has chosen Jesus to one day be Lord and Ruler over all created things.

Within Jesus resides the prototype—the seed—of the church. When He turns thirty, He begins the ministry for which He was sent to earth. Jesus is baptized in the Jordan River and begins preaching the Kingdom of God.[1] His message is essentially "repent," that is, change your allegiance because the Kingdom of God has come and Satan's sovereignty is about to be overthrown. Take your loyalty away from Satan's kingdom, his representatives, and his institutions and put it in God.

Jesus calls twelve men to live with Him for three and a half years. During this time, He will display to the Twelve the life of His Father's Kingdom.

---

[1] Mark 1:15; Luke 4:43; 8:1.

The life of the Kingdom is the life of the age to come.[2] It is the life of a new order—a new civilization. It is eternal life. This life belongs to a different age. It existed in the age before creation and it will be fully manifested at the end of this age when Jesus rules the universe. But this life is available to men today, because the Kingdom of God is here in the Person of Jesus.

Day and night, through various and sundry circumstances, the Twelve behold a Man who is showing them the life of the Kingdom of God. Greater still, they behold the very *embodiment* of that Kingdom in human flesh![3]

Jesus Christ is the incarnation—the infleshment—of the Kingdom of God. He makes it visible. Consequently, wherever Jesus is, there is the Kingdom. Wherever Jesus travels, God's rule is present. Wherever Jesus walks, the kingdom of darkness is thrust out. Wherever Jesus works, the coming age breaks into space-time.

As Jesus ministers all throughout Galilee, He performs the works of the Kingdom. The works of the Kingdom include bringing life to the dead, healing the sick, setting captives free, and delivering the demon-possessed.[4] The works of the Kingdom prove that the Kingdom of God has come as a present reality in the midst of an evil age.

Even though the old fallen age continues on, the Kingdom of God has invaded the realm of Satan to deliver men and

---

[2] The Kingdom is often described as "the age (or world) to come"(Matt. 12:32; Mark 10:29-30; Luke 20:34-36; Eph. 1:21; Heb. 6:5) over against this present age (Matt. 13:22, 39, 49-50; 24:3; Gal. 1:4; 2 Cor. 4:3-4; Rom. 12:2; Eph. 2:1-2).

[3] Luke 17:20-21.

[4] Matt. 4:23; 12:28; Luke 4:18-21; 9:11; 10:9; 11:20.

women from his rule. The Kingdom of God is here! It lives and breathes in Jesus of Nazareth. And men and women are violently pressing into it.[5]

The Twelve live in community—sharing their lives together. They recognize that God the Father has chosen Jesus to be both Lord and King. Consequently, they live under Christ's rule just as Jesus lives under the Father's rule. In this way, Jesus and the Twelve constitute the embryo of the church.

Jesus trains the Twelve to continue His ministry when He leaves the earth. That ministry is to proclaim the Kingdom of God, do the works of the Kingdom, and to duplicate the communal life of the Kingdom that they are experiencing in Galilee with Jesus.[6] The goal of the Kingdom of God is to create communities that live by the life of the Kingdom and express it in the earth.[7]

---

[5] Matt. 11:12; Luke 12:31-32; 16:16.
[6] Luke 9:2; 10:9, 11.
[7] This chapter is an extremely concise summary of the four Gospels.

OBSERVATIONS

Jesus Christ is Lord and King of the community of the Twelve. There is no shepherd or pastor but Him. The Twelve meet together informally in homes as well as in out-door settings. They do not gather together in a sacred building. Their meetings are not marked by a liturgy or order of worship.

Jesus does not found a seminary or a Bible school. He trains the Twelve by living with them, showing them the conduct of the Kingdom through day-to-day, real-life activities. The Twelve watch Him proclaim the Kingdom and do the works of the Kingdom.

In Jesus, the Twelve are beholding the new creation which has burst forth in the midst of the old creation. In Jesus, the will of heaven—the unseen realm where God rules—is being done upon earth.

And He said to them, "I tell you the truth, some who are standing here will not taste death before they see the Kingdom of God come with power."
-Mark 9:1

CHAPTER 2

THE KINGDOM COMES TO JERUSALEM
A.D. 30 - A.D. 41

Jesus of Nazareth has died and risen again, and God the Father has made Him both Lord and Christ (the Anointed One). Jesus sends the Twelve to continue His work of declaring and expressing the Kingdom of God. But He asks them to wait in Jerusalem until they are empowered by the Holy Spirit.

Jesus spends six weeks with His disciples, speaking to them about the Kingdom of God.[1] He then ascends into heaven.

Ten days later the day of Pentecost arrives. In a violent spasm, the Kingdom of God comes to earth in the Person of the Holy Spirit. 120 disciples of Jesus are baptized into Christ and form His Body. What was an embryo in Galilee is born in Jerusalem. The future invades the present. Tomorrow meets today. The age to come enters the present age. The heavens have kissed the earth, and the Kingdom of God takes up residence in the 120!

Over the next seven years, the Twelve preach the Kingdom of God. Their message is simple: "God has made Jesus both Lord and Christ (the Anointed One)."[2]

---

[1] Acts 1:3.
[2] Acts 2:36.

Thousands of Jews receive Jesus Christ as Lord and are added to the church. They, too, possess the life of the Kingdom and they display it in Jerusalem. Within one year after its birth, the church in Jerusalem contains about 10,000 people. Those in the church live in community—sharing their lives together. They have surrendered to the rule of the Kingdom. They fellowship with Jesus Christ and with one another. Every day, the believers meet in homes all throughout the city. They also gather together in a large porch on the east side of the temple called "Solomon's Porch" to hear the twelve apostles preach.

The Twelve, who have lived with Jesus for three and a half years, preach Jesus Christ to the Jews in Jerusalem. Certain men in the church are developing in both spiritual life and spiritual gifts. They are prophets, teachers, evangelists, and apostles. Among them are: Stephen, Philip, Agabus, Silas, Barnabas, and James (the Lord's half-brother).

The Kingdom of God spreads in Jerusalem and begins clashing with the kingdom of darkness. The apostles are being persecuted by the Jewish leaders in the city. Stephen begins to preach Christ in one of the synagogues in Jerusalem. Out of jealousy, the Jews stone Stephen to death. Stephen is the church's first martyr.

Paul of Tarsus (whose Jewish name is Saul) is one of the Pharisees responsible for Stephen's death. Paul launches an unbridled assault on the church. With the exception of the Twelve, the entire church in Jerusalem leaves the city to flee the persecution. The church scatters and migrates to Judea, Galilee, and Samaria. The scattered believers share Christ with the Jews in those regions. The Kingdom of God now spreads throughout Palestine.[3] The Twelve travel to the new churches in Palestine, encouraging them and building them up.

On his way to Damascus, Paul has a head-on-collision with Jesus Christ and submits to His rulership. In blinding light, Jesus appears to Paul, and Paul is converted.

Jesus calls Paul to be an apostle to the Gentiles. Paul gathers with the church in Damascus, which is one of the churches that was transplanted when the church in Jerusalem scattered.

Paul immediately begins preaching in the synagogues in Damascus. He then vanishes into Arabia for approximately three years. In Arabia, the Lord Jesus gives Paul a revelation of the gospel of grace. Paul returns to Damascus and resumes preaching in the synagogues. The Jews plot to kill him so he escapes to Jerusalem.

While in Jerusalem, Paul meets Peter and James. Paul begins preaching in the Jerusalem synagogues and the Jews try to kill him. So he returns to his home town in Tarsus, Cilicia and disappears for a time from the saga. The churches in Judea, Galilee, and Samaria enjoy peace and spiritual prosperity.

Peter, the apostle, travels to Caesarea and brings the gospel to a group of Gentiles there. A church is born, and the Kingdom of God comes to Caesarea.

Meanwhile, the church in Jerusalem has repopulated itself. A large number of Jewish priests become Christians and are added to the church. These men make up "the circumcision

---

[3] Acts 8:12.

party." The circumcision party believes that in order to be saved, a Gentile must believe in Jesus *and* be circumcised.[4]

---

[4] This chapter is a summary of Acts 1:1-11:18.

OBSERVATIONS

When Christ was on earth, the Kingdom of God only dwelt in one Man—Jesus of Nazareth. And it was limited by time and space. On the day of Pentecost, the Kingdom extended to the church. Just as Christ embodied the Kingdom in the days of His flesh, the church now embodies the Kingdom—for the church is the Body of Christ returned to earth.

The Holy Spirit has come to earth and has translated all who believe in the Lord Jesus from the kingdom of darkness into the Kingdom of God.[5] Those who believe are made residents of a new realm where Jesus, and not Caesar, is King.[6] The church in Jerusalem, along with the churches throughout Palestine, have no shepherd or pastor but Jesus Christ. After more than a decade, elders (plural) emerge in the church of Jerusalem and care for the flock. But there will not be a single or head pastor who does all the ministry or makes decisions for the church.

The churches meet together informally in homes as well as in out-door settings like Solomon's porch. They do not gather together in a sacred building. Their meetings are not marked by a liturgy or order of worship. There is no seminary or Bible college. Just as Jesus trained the Twelve, so the Twelve are unwittingly training Stephen, Barnabas, Silas, Agabus, Philip, etc. The Twelve proclaim the Kingdom of God and do the works of the Kingdom. These other men follow suit in the years to come.[7] The church is a new creation

---

[5] Col. 1:13.
[6] Php. 3:20.
[7] E.g., Philip—Acts 8:12.

from heaven that has burst forth into the earth in the midst of the old creation.

Therefore I tell you [Jews] that the Kingdom of God will be taken away from you and given to a people [Gentiles] who will produce its fruit.

-Matthew 21:43

CHAPTER 3

THE KINGDOM COMES TO ANTIOCH
A.D. 41 - A.D. 47

Some of the Christians that were scattered from the Jerusalem church make their way to a Gentile city called Antioch in Syria. Some of them preach the Kingdom to the Gentiles in that city. As a result, many Gentiles come to Christ and a predominantly Gentile church is born in Antioch. The Kingdom of God has been given to the Gentiles!

The church in Jerusalem sends Barnabas to Antioch to see the new church. After arriving, Barnabas travels to Tarsus, Cilicia and looks for Paul. He brings Paul back to Antioch to help him care for the church there. In the years to come, Barnabas will train Paul to be a messenger of the Kingdom just as the Twelve trained Barnabas to preach the Kingdom. Luke and Titus are two Gentiles who belong to the church in Antioch.

As the Kingdom of God gains strength, the kingdom of darkness retaliates. A famine hits Judea and the Jerusalem Christians suffer severely. However, the church in Antioch sends financial relief to the church in Jerusalem. James the apostle is martyred and Peter is put in prison awaiting execution. The church in Jerusalem touches God's throne with prayer and the Lord miraculously delivers Peter from prison.

During the next six years of the church's life in Antioch, prophets and teachers emerge. Paul and Barnabas are among them. The Holy Spirit directs some in the church to send out Paul and Barnabas to the work of preaching the Kingdom and establishing churches in other lands.[1]

---

[1] This chapter is a summary of Acts 11:19-12:25.

OBSERVATIONS

The twelve apostles begin traveling and raising up churches in other cities. Whenever they plant or strengthen a church, they leave that church on their own. They do not reside in it to pastor it.

The church in Antioch grows rapidly. It is the largest Gentile church on earth. Antioch is the summary witness that the Kingdom, which was first promised to the Jews, has been given to the Gentiles also.

The church in Antioch has no shepherd or pastor but Jesus Christ. Over the first six years of its life, prophets and teachers emerge in the church. But there is no one person who takes charge. Jesus Christ is Head and King in the church at Antioch!

The church meets together informally in homes throughout Antioch. It does not gather together in a sacred building. The meetings of the church are not marked by a liturgy or order of worship. There is no seminary or Bible college. Barnabas has been training Paul for the Lord's work.

Just as the Father sent Jesus, and Jesus sent the Twelve, the Holy Spirit sends Paul and Barnabas to the work of expanding the Kingdom through planting churches.

They preached the good news in that city and won a large number of disciples. Then they returned to Lystra, Iconium and Antioch, strengthening the disciples and encouraging them to remain true to the faith. "We must go through many hardships to enter the Kingdom of God," they said.
-Acts 14:21-22

CHAPTER 4

THE KINGDOM COMES TO GALATIA
A.D. 47 - A.D. 50

Barnabas and Paul leave Antioch of Syria and bring the gospel of the Kingdom to the Island of Cyprus. John Mark, Barnabas' young cousin, serves the two men on the trip.

From Cyprus, they head to the region of South Galatia where they preach the Kingdom of God. As a result, the two apostles plant four churches in four cities of South Galatia: Antioch of Pisidia, Iconium, Lystra, and Derbe. (Before the men get to South Galatia, John Mark returns home to Jerusalem.)

These churches are predominantly Gentile, though they contain some Jews. Paul and Barnabas return to Antioch of Syria and give the church a report of God's work among the Gentiles in South Galatia. The two men rest in the church of Antioch, Syria for about a year.

Back in Rome, Emperor Claudius issues a decree expelling all Jews from the city of Rome. A Roman Jew named Aquila and his wife Priscilla are among them. This couple moves to Corinth.

Peter visits the church in Antioch. Some of the circumcision party in Jerusalem come to Antioch and tell the Gentile Christians they must be circumcised and follow the Law of Moses. They also persuade Peter not to eat with the Gentile Christians. When Paul takes note of this, he rebukes Peter publicly.

Peter returns to Jerusalem and gives a report on Paul's work among the Gentiles in South Galatia. Upon hearing the report, some in the circumcision party in Jerusalem head to South Galatia. When they arrive, they tell the four Gentile churches that they must be circumcised and follow the Law of Moses to be saved. They tell them that Paul is not a real apostle because he did not come from Jerusalem, that he is a man-pleaser, and that he rebuked the chief apostle, Peter. When Paul gets word of this, he writes a letter to the four Galatian churches.

Galatians

OUTLINE:

Apology: Defending the Gospel of Grace.
Chapters 1-2

Argument: Declaring the Gospel of Grace.
Chapters 3-4

Appeal: Defining the Life of Grace.
Chapters 5-6

KINGDOM QUOTES:

Gal. 1:3: Grace and peace to you from God our Father and THE LORD JESUS CHRIST.

Gal. 5:21: . . . drunkenness, orgies, and the like. I warn you, as I did before, that those who live like this will not inherit THE KINGDOM OF GOD.

Gal. 6:14: May I never boast except in the cross of OUR LORD JESUS CHRIST, through which the world has been crucified to me, and I to the world.

Gal. 6:18: The grace of OUR LORD JESUS CHRIST be with your spirit, brothers. Amen.

In Antioch, there is a hot debate between the circumcision party from Jerusalem and Paul and Barnabas over the issue of circumcision.

The church in Antioch decides to send Paul and Barnabas to Jerusalem to see if the Jerusalem church and the twelve apostles agree with the circumcision party over the matter.

When Paul and Barnabas arrive in Jerusalem, the issue is debated by the entire church. The apostles, elders, and entire church in Jerusalem decide that the Gentile believers do not have to be circumcised or obey the Law of Moses. But it is agreed that they should follow four Jewish restrictions.

Back in Palestine, the dispersed Jewish believers are suffering persecution from those in the kingdom of darkness. They are being oppressed by the rich and letting their hearts go after the kingdoms of this world.

They have also heard a perverted form of Paul's gospel of grace and have concluded that it is a license to sin. After hearing about the Jerusalem council, they mistakenly conclude that the twelve apostles agree with this corrupted version of the gospel. To address this problem, James, the

Lord's half-brother, writes a letter to the scattered Jewish Christians.[1]

James

OUTLINE:

Faith and Temptation: Working Patience.
Chapter 1

Faith and Love: Good Works.
Chapter 2

Faith and Wisdom: Fruitful Speech.
Chapter 3

Faith and Purity: Godly Character.
Chapters 4-5

KINGDOM QUOTES:

Jam. 1:1: James, a servant of God and of THE LORD JESUS CHRIST, to the twelve tribes scattered among the nations: Greetings.

Jam. 2:1: My brothers, as believers in OUR GLORIOUS LORD JESUS CHRIST, don't show favoritism.

---

[1] This chapter is a summary of Acts 13:1-15:35, Galatians, and James.

Jam. 2:5: Listen, my dear brothers: Has not God chosen those who are poor in the eyes of the world to be rich in faith and to inherit THE KINGDOM HE PROMISED THOSE WHO LOVE HIM?

OBSERVATIONS

Paul and Barnabas plant four Gentile churches in South Galatia in a very short period of time. They then leave those churches on their own. They do not reside in them to pastor them. The four Gentile churches are enjoying the life of the Kingdom of God. The churches in Antioch of Pisidia, Iconium, Lystra and Derbe have no shepherd or pastor but Jesus Christ, the King of kings and Lord of lords. More than one year after they arrive in South Galatia, Paul and Barnabas select elders (plural) to care for the churches. However, the elders do not rule or dominate the churches. They simply provide oversight.

The churches gather informally in homes. They are joyfully enthroning Jesus Christ. As a result, they are experiencing the joy, peace, and righteousness that is part of the Kingdom.[2] The believers are living in the presence of the future—"tasting the powers of the age to come."[3]

The church in Jerusalem has a church debate to resolve the matter of whether or not the Gentiles must be circumcised and obey the Law of Moses. Everyone in the church freely shares his mind. The entire church, with the leadership of the elders and the twelve apostles, comes to a decision. The decision was not made by a pastor or special board of men. It was made by all the brothers and sisters in the church and approved by the Holy Spirit.[4]

---

[2] Rom. 14:17.
[3] Heb. 6:5.
[4] Acts 15:22, 25, 28.

All this is evidence that God's judgment is right, and as a result you will be counted worthy of the Kingdom of God, for which you are suffering.
    -2 Thessalonians 1:5

CHAPTER 5

THE KINGDOM COMES TO GREECE
A.D. 50 - A.D. 53

Paul and Barnabas have an irreconcilable disagreement over whether or not to take John Mark on their next trip. So the two men part ways. Barnabas and John Mark go to Cyprus. Paul and Silas (from Jerusalem) revisit the churches in South Galatia and check on their progress.

When Paul and Silas come to Lystra, they take Timothy with them on their journey. (Timothy is a young respected brother in the church.)

Paul, Silas, and Timothy head to Northern Greece (Macedonia) and they preach the Kingdom in the cities of Philippi, Thessalonica, and Berea. The two men plant churches in all of those cities. And in each one, Paul and Silas are persecuted. Because they preach the Kingdom of God and the Lordship of Christ, they are charged with preaching another King other than Caesar. This charge gets Paul and Silas jailed and flogged in Philippi and it gets Paul thrown out of Thessalonica.

In Berea, Paul receives opposition and the believers secretly send him off to Athens in Southern Greece (Achaia) where he preaches the Kingdom. In Athens, Paul's message is rejected. Silas and Timothy rejoin Paul in Athens. Paul desires to visit the church in Thessalonica, but Satan thwarts him. So he sends Timothy to Thessalonica and Silas to Philippi.

Paul comes to the city of Corinth in fear and trembling. He will spend eighteen months in the city of Corinth, preaching the Kingdom of God and planting a church. Priscilla and Aquila are part of the church in Corinth. Like Paul, they are tentmakers.

While Paul is working with the church in Corinth, he does not take any money from it. Instead, he pays his own way, working with his hands as a tentmaker.

Silas and Timothy meet Paul in Corinth. Timothy tells Paul that the Thessalonican believers are in crisis. They are being persecuted by hostile neighbors who oppose their belief that Jesus is King. Someone in the church has died, and there are questions about what happens to Christians when they pass away. Paul writes 1 Thessalonians to address these issues.

1 Thessalonians

OUTLINE:

Faith: Turning from the Old.
Chapters 1-2

Labor: Serving in the New.
Chapters 3:1-4:12

Patience: Waiting on His Return.
Chapters 4:13-5:28

KINGDOM QUOTES:

1 Thess. 1:1: Paul, Silas and Timothy, to the church of the Thessalonians in God the Father and THE LORD JESUS CHRIST: Grace and peace to you.

1 Thess. 1:3: We continually remember before our God and Father your work produced by faith, your labor prompted by love, and your endurance inspired by hope in OUR LORD JESUS CHRIST.

1 Thess. 2:12: . . . encouraging, comforting and urging you to live lives worthy of God, who calls you into HIS KINGDOM and glory.

1 Thess. 2:15: . . . who killed THE LORD JESUS and the prophets and also drove us out. They displease God and are hostile to all men.

1 Thess. 2:19 : For what is our hope, our joy, or the crown in which we will glory in the presence of OUR LORD JESUS when He comes? Is it not you?

1 Thess. 3:11: Now may our God and Father Himself and OUR LORD JESUS clear the way for us to come to you.

1 Thess. 3:13: May He strengthen your hearts so that you will be blameless and holy in the presence of our God and Father when OUR LORD JESUS comes with all His holy ones.

1 Thess. 4:1: Finally, brothers, we instructed you how to live in order to please God, as in fact you are living. Now we ask you and urge you in THE LORD JESUS to do this more and more.

1 Thess. 4:2: For you know what instructions we gave you by THE AUTHORITY OF THE LORD JESUS.

1 Thess. 5:9: For God did not appoint us to suffer wrath but to receive salvation through OUR LORD JESUS CHRIST.

1 Thess. 5:23: May God Himself, the God of peace, sanctify you through and through. May your whole spirit, soul and body be kept blameless at the coming of OUR LORD JESUS CHRIST.

1 Thess. 5:28: The grace of OUR LORD JESUS CHRIST be with you.

Not long after Paul sends 1 Thessalonians, the church in Thessalonica is enduring another problem. Some of the men have misinterpreted Paul's letter to mean that Jesus is going to set up His Kingdom at any moment. As a result, some in the church quit their jobs and begin living off the other believers. When Paul gets word of this, he writes a second letter to the church in Thessalonica.

2 Thessalonians

OUTLINE:

Consolation: The Revelation of Jesus Christ.
Chapter 1

Instruction: The Day of the Lord.
Chapter 2:1-12

Exhortation: The Present Duty.
Chapters 2:12-3:18

KINGDOM QUOTES:

2 Thess. 1:1: Paul, Silas and Timothy, to the church of the Thessalonians in God our Father and THE LORD JESUS CHRIST.

2 Thess. 1:2: Grace and peace to you from God the Father and THE LORD JESUS CHRIST.

2 Thess. 1:5: All this is evidence that God's judgment is right, and as a result you will be counted worthy of THE KINGDOM OF GOD, for which you are suffering.

2 Thess. 1:7: . . . and give relief to you who are troubled, and to us as well. This will happen when THE LORD JESUS is revealed from heaven in blazing fire with His powerful angels.

2 Thess. 1:8: He will punish those who do not know God and do not obey the gospel of OUR LORD JESUS.

2 Thess. 1:9: They will be punished with everlasting destruction and shut out from the presence of the Lord and FROM THE MAJESTY OF HIS POWER.

2 Thess. 1:12: We pray this so that the name of OUR LORD JESUS may be glorified in you, and you in Him, according to the grace of our God and THE LORD JESUS CHRIST.

2 Thess. 2:1: Concerning the coming of OUR LORD JESUS Christ and our being gathered to Him . . .

2 Thess. 2:8: And then the lawless one will be revealed, whom THE LORD JESUS will overthrow with the breath of His mouth and destroy by the splendor of His coming.

2 Thess. 2:14: He called you to this through our gospel, that you might share in the glory of OUR LORD JESUS CHRIST.

2 Thess. 2:16: May OUR LORD JESUS CHRIST Himself and God our Father, who loved us and by His grace gave us eternal encouragement and good hope . . .

2 Thess. 3:6: In the name of THE LORD JESUS CHRIST, we command you, brothers, to keep away from every brother who is idle and does not live according to the teaching you received from us.

2 Thess. 3:12: Such people we command and urge in THE LORD JESUS CHRIST to settle down and earn the bread they eat.

2 Thess. 3:18: The grace of OUR LORD JESUS CHRIST be with you all.

Paul endures minor opposition in Corinth, but God keeps him from harm. His ministry as a whole in the city is fruitful. After eighteen months, he leaves for Ephesus with Priscilla and Aquila.

When he arrives in Ephesus, Paul preaches the Kingdom in the synagogue of the Jews for a very short time. He then leaves to visit Jerusalem and heads back to Antioch of Syria. Priscilla and Aquila wait for him to return to Ephesus.[1]

---

[1] This chapter is a summary of Acts 15:36-18:22, 1 Thessalonians, and 2 Thessalonians.

OBSERVATIONS

Paul and Silas plant four Gentile churches in Greece in a very short period of time. They then leave those churches on their own. They do not reside in them to pastor them.

The four Gentile churches are enjoying and expressing the Kingdom of God. The churches in Philippi, Thessalonica, Berea, and Corinth have no shepherd or pastor but Jesus Christ, the King of kings and Lord of lords.

These churches do not erect special buildings to meet in. They do not have an order of worship every time they gather. Instead, every member is free to function as the Spirit of God leads.[2] The church is led by the brothers and the sisters under the Kingship of Jesus Christ, not by any man. When Paul writes his two letters to the church in Thessalonica, he addresses the entire church and asks them to resolve their own problems.

---

[2] See 1 Cor. 14.

Paul entered the synagogue [in Ephesus] and spoke boldly there for three months, arguing persuasively about the Kingdom of God.
-Acts 19:8

CHAPTER 6

THE KINGDOM COMES TO EPHESUS
A.D. 54 - A.D. 58

In Ephesus, Priscilla and Aquila meet a man named Apollos. Apollos is a Jew from Alexandria, Egypt. He is a Christian, but he is not clear on the gospel. Priscilla and Aquila give Apollos a clearer understanding of the gospel. Apollos leaves Ephesus and pays a visit to the church in Corinth. Peter also visits Corinth.

Paul arrives in Ephesus with six men from the churches he has planted. Paul's plan is to train these men to proclaim the Kingdom of God and plant churches. He will train these men just as Jesus trained the Twelve. These six men are: Titus of Antioch, Timothy of Lystra, Gaius of Derbe, Sopater of Berea, Aristarchus and Secundus of Thessalonica.

Paul preaches the Kingdom of God for three months in the Jewish synagogue.[1] The Jews oppose him so he leaves the synagogue. Paul then rents the Hall of Tyrannus to preach, teach, and train his young apprentices. Two men are converted (Tychicus and Trophimus), and they are added to the number of apprentices that Paul is training.

Paul will spend a total of three years in Ephesus, preaching the Kingdom of God to all who will hear him.[2] He is also training eight men for the work of proclaiming the Kingdom

---

[1] Acts 19:8.
[2] Acts 20:25.

and planting churches. The church in Ephesus is strong and expresses the Kingdom of God in the city.

While in Ephesus, Paul leads a man named Philemon to the Lord. (Philemon owns a slave named Onesimus.) Paul also leads a man named Epaphras to Christ. Both Philemon and Epaphras are from Colosse.

There is much spiritual opposition in the city—a conflict between the kingdom of darkness and the Kingdom of God. It is so intense that Paul falls into despair.

Nonetheless, he exhibits the power of the Kingdom of God by signs and wonders. Sweat rags are taken from him and they are used to heal sicknesses and drive out demons.

A woman from the church in Corinth named Chloe visits Paul in Ephesus and gives him a report about the Corinthian church. The church is in severe crisis. It is dividing into four fragments, there is strife among the believers, civil disputes, sexual immorality, chaotic meetings, drunkenness and gluttony at the Lord's Supper, and other perils.

Shortly thereafter, three men from the Corinthian church bring Paul a letter filled with practical questions. Some of the questions have to do with marriage, divorce, eating meat offered to idols, dining in pagan temples, women's head coverings, and the future resurrection. In response, Paul writes a letter to the church which addresses the crisis and answers the church's questions.

1 Corinthians

OUTLINE:

Correction: Exposing the Fleshly.
Chapters 1-11

Construction: Encouraging the Spiritual.
Chapters 12-14

KINGDOM QUOTES:

1 Cor. 1:2: To the church of God in Corinth, to those sanctified in Christ Jesus and called to be holy, together with all those everywhere who call on the name of our LORD JESUS CHRIST—THEIR LORD AND OURS.

1 Cor. 1:3: Grace and peace to you from God our Father and THE LORD JESUS CHRIST.

1 Cor. 1:7: Therefore you do not lack any spiritual gift as you eagerly wait for OUR LORD JESUS CHRIST to be revealed.

1 Cor. 1:8 : He will keep you strong to the end, so that you will be blameless on the day of OUR LORD JESUS CHRIST.

1 Cor. 1:9: God, who has called you into fellowship with His Son JESUS CHRIST OUR LORD, is faithful.

1 Cor. 1:10: I appeal to you, brothers, in the name of OUR LORD JESUS CHRIST, that all of you agree with one another so that there may be no divisions among you and that you may be perfectly united in mind and thought.

1 Cor. 4:20: For THE KINGDOM OF GOD is not a matter of talk but of power.

1 Cor. 5:4: When you are assembled in the name of OUR LORD JESUS and I am with you in spirit, and the power of OUR LORD JESUS is present . . .

1 Cor. 6:9: Do you not know that the wicked will not inherit THE KINGDOM OF GOD?

1 Cor. 6:11: And that is what some of you were. But you were washed, you were sanctified, you were justified in the name of THE LORD JESUS CHRIST and by the Spirit of our God.

1 Cor. 8:6: Yet for us there is but one God, the Father, from whom all things came and for whom we live; and there is but ONE LORD, JESUS CHRIST, through whom all things came and through whom we live.

1 Cor. 9:1: Am I not free? Am I not an apostle? Have I not seen JESUS OUR LORD? Are you not the result of my work in the Lord?

1 Cor. 11:3: Now I want you to realize that the HEAD OF EVERY MAN IS CHRIST . . .

1 Cor. 11:23: For I received from the Lord what I also passed on to you: THE LORD JESUS, on the night He was betrayed, took bread . . .

1 Cor. 12:3: Therefore I tell you that no one who is speaking by the Spirit of God says, "Jesus be cursed," and no one can say, "JESUS IS LORD," except by the Holy Spirit.

1 Cor. 15:24-25: Then the end will come, when He hands over the KINGDOM TO GOD THE FATHER AFTER HE HAS DESTROYED ALL DOMINION, AUTHORITY, AND POWER. FOR HE MUST REIGN UNTIL HE HAS PUT ALL HIS ENEMIES UNDER HIS FEET.

1 Cor. 15:31: I die every day—I mean that, brothers—just as surely as I glory over you in CHRIST JESUS OUR LORD.

1 Cor. 15:50: I declare to you, brothers, that flesh and blood cannot inherit THE KINGDOM OF GOD, nor does the perishable inherit the imperishable.

1 Cor. 15:57 But thanks be to God! He gives us the victory through OUR LORD JESUS CHRIST.

1 Cor. 16:23: The grace of THE LORD JESUS be with you.

Paul wishes to see the Kingdom of God break into the Eternal City—Rome. So he sends Priscilla and Aquila back to Rome. He also sends word to all the Gentile churches he has planted and asks some in each church to move to Rome.

As a result, the church in Rome is born. It is a church that has been transplanted from other churches that Paul has planted. The Kingdom of God has arrived in Rome!

Paul sends his apprentices to preach the Kingdom and plant churches all over Asia Minor. Accordingly, churches are born in Smyrna, Thyatira, Sardis, Philadelphia, and Pergamum.

Upon hearing that his first letter to the Corinthians has been rejected, Paul pays an urgent visit to Corinth. While he is there, someone opposes Paul and the church does not stand with the apostle. Paul leaves hurt and writes a scathing letter to the church. Titus brings the letter to Corinth. Yet as soon as Titus leaves to deliver the letter, Paul regrets that he wrote it and fears that it will cause more damage than good.[3]

The kingdom of darkness gains strength in Ephesus. The silversmiths of the city, along with the local Jews, oppose Paul severely. A riot occurs as a result.

To escape the conflict, Paul leaves Ephesus and heads to Macedonia. While in Macedonia, his heart is full of anxiety over the letter he wrote to the Corinthian church. He seeks for Titus to find out how the Corinthians received the letter.

Back in Colosse, Epaphras plants three churches in his home region: A church in Colosse, a church in Laodicea, and a church in Hierapolis. The Kingdom of God is spreading throughout Asia Minor.

Paul finds Titus and receives good news that his scathing letter to the church in Corinth was well received. But the church is experiencing another crisis. Some Jews from Jerusalem are trying to take over the church. Their tactic is to malign Paul's character and ministry.

The church has also dropped the ball on collecting for the relief fund that Paul wishes to take to Jerusalem to help the poor believers there. To address these issues, Paul writes another letter to the Corinthians.

---

[3] Paul makes mention of this letter in 2 Corinthians, but it is lost to us.

2 Corinthians

OUTLINE:

Ministry: Against the Law of Moses.
Chapters 1-7

Stewardship: Against a Spirit of Self-Serving.
Chapters 8-9

Conflict: Against the Kingdom of Darkness.
Chapters 10-13

KINGDOM QUOTES:

2 Cor. 1:2: Grace and peace to you from God our Father and THE LORD JESUS CHRIST.

2 Cor. 1:3: Praise be to the God and Father of OUR LORD JESUS CHRIST, the Father of compassion and the God of all comfort.

2 Cor. 1:14: . . . as you have understood us in part, you will come to understand fully that you can boast of us just as we will boast of you in the day of THE LORD JESUS.

2 Cor. 4:5: For we do not preach ourselves, but JESUS CHRIST AS LORD, and ourselves as your servants for Jesus' sake.

2 Cor. 4:14: Because we know that the one who raised THE LORD JESUS from the dead will also raise us with Jesus and present us with you in His presence.

2 Cor. 8:9: For you know the grace of OUR LORD JESUS CHRIST, that though He was rich, yet for your sakes He became poor, so that you through His poverty might become rich.

2 Cor. 11:31: The God and Father of THE LORD JESUS, who is to be praised forever, knows that I am not lying.

2 Cor. 13:14: May the grace of THE LORD JESUS CHRIST, and the love of God, and the fellowship of the Holy Spirit be with you all.

Paul leaves Macedonia and preaches the Kingdom of God in Illyricum (Dalmatia). He then winters in Corinth. While in Corinth, Paul gets word that the church in Rome is having problems. There is tension between the Jewish believers and the Gentile believers in the church. They are divided over what foods should be eaten and what days should be set apart as holy.

The church also asks Paul to pen a treatise on the gospel for the visitors who have come to the Lord in Rome and then leave the city. In response, Paul writes a letter to the Roman Christians.

Romans

OUTLINE:

Salvation: Justified from Sins.
Chapters 1:1-5:11

Sanctification: Delivered from Sin.
Chapters 5:12-8:39

Incorporation: The Jew and Gentile in God's Plan.
Chapters 9-11

Transformation: Life in the Body.
Chapters 12-16

KINGDOM QUOTES:

Rom. 1:4: . . . declared with power to be the Son of God by His resurrection from the dead: JESUS CHRIST OUR LORD.

Rom. 1:7: To all in Rome who are loved by God and called to be saints: Grace and peace to you from God our Father and from THE LORD JESUS CHRIST.

Rom. 4:24: But also for us, to whom God will credit righteousness—for us who believe in Him who raised JESUS OUR LORD from the dead.

Rom. 5:1: Therefore, since we have been justified through faith, we have peace with God through OUR LORD JESUS CHRIST.

Rom. 5:11: Not only is this so, but we also rejoice in God through OUR LORD JESUS CHRIST, through whom we have now received reconciliation.

Rom. 5:17: For if, by the trespass of the one man, death reigned through that one man, how much more will those who receive God's abundant provision of grace and of the gift of righteousness REIGN IN LIFE through the one Man, Jesus Christ.

Rom. 5:21: So that, just as sin reigned in death, so also grace might reign through righteousness to bring eternal life through JESUS CHRIST OUR LORD.

Rom. 6:23: For the wages of sin is death, but the gift of God is eternal life in CHRIST JESUS OUR LORD.

Rom. 7:25: Thanks be to God—through JESUS CHRIST OUR LORD!

Rom. 8:39: Neither height nor depth, nor anything else in all creation, will be able to separate us from the love of God that is in CHRIST JESUS OUR LORD.

Rom. 10:9: That if you confess with your mouth, "JESUS IS LORD," and believe in your heart that God raised Him from the dead, you will be saved.

Rom. 10:12: For there is no difference between Jew and Gentile—THE SAME LORD IS LORD OF ALL and richly blesses all who call on Him.

Rom. 13:14: Rather, clothe yourselves with THE LORD JESUS CHRIST, and do not think about how to gratify the desires of the sinful nature.

Rom. 14:9: For this very reason, Christ died and returned to life SO THAT HE MIGHT BE THE LORD OF BOTH THE DEAD AND THE LIVING.

Rom. 14:14: As one who is in THE LORD JESUS, I am fully convinced that no food is unclean in itself.

Rom. 14:17: For THE KINGDOM OF GOD is not a matter of eating and drinking, but of righteousness, peace and joy in the Holy Spirit,

Rom. 15:6: So that with one heart and mouth you may glorify the God and Father of OUR LORD JESUS CHRIST.

Rom. 15:12: And again, Isaiah says, "The Root of Jesse will spring up, one who will arise TO RULE OVER THE NATIONS; the Gentiles will hope in Him."

Rom. 15:30: I urge you, brothers, by OUR LORD JESUS CHRIST and by the love of the Spirit, to join me in my struggle by praying to God for me.

Rom. 16:18: For such people are not serving OUR LORD CHRIST, but their own appetites. By smooth talk and flattery they deceive the minds of naive people.

Rom. 16:20: The God of peace will soon crush Satan under your feet. The grace of OUR LORD JESUS be with you.

After three months in Corinth, Paul visits Macedonia and then heads off to Miletus. In Miletus, he meets with the elders in the church of Ephesus and bids them farewell.

Paul and his eight apprentices head toward Jerusalem. They bring a large sum of money that has been collected from all the Gentile churches that Paul has planted. The money is a gift to the Jerusalem church to relieve them of their poverty. It is Paul's hope that the relief fund will heal the tension that exists between the Jewish and Gentile churches.

While Paul is in Jerusalem, the Jews falsely accuse him of blaspheming the temple. A riot ensues, and the Jews try to kill Paul. The Romans immediately seize Paul, and throw him in jail. Some Jews plot to kill him while he is in jail. When the Roman guards get word of it, they send Paul away by night to Caesarea.[4]

---

[4] This chapter is a summary of Acts 18:23-23:35, 1 Corinthians, 2 Corinthians, and Romans with added material from Colossians and Philemon.

OBSERVATIONS

Paul plants one church in Ephesus and stays in the city for three years to train men. He then leaves the church on its own. He does not reside in it to pastor it. While in Ephesus, Paul does not found a seminary or Bible college. Instead, he trains men the same way that Jesus trained the Twelve. The men live with Paul for three years and watch him proclaim the Kingdom and do the works of the Kingdom. Paul transplants a church in Rome by sending people to it from other churches.

The churches in Ephesus and Rome are enjoying and expressing the Kingdom of God. Neither church has a pastor. They only have Jesus Christ to lead them. Christ is the only Head of the Body, the King of kings and Lord of lords.

After three years, elders emerge in the church of Ephesus. But those elders are overseers; they do not rule the church nor do they do all the ministry. According to Paul, they are *among* the flock, not *over* the flock.[5]

In Ephesus, Paul rents a lecture hall (the Hall of Tyrannus) to conduct the work of preaching the Kingdom and training his apprentices. (This hall is used for the meetings of *the work*, not for the meetings of *the church*.)[6]

The churches do not erect special buildings in which to meet. They hold their church meetings in homes.[7] The church meetings in Ephesus and Rome are marked by every-member

---

[5] Acts 20:28, NASB.

[6] See *Who is Your Covering?* (Chapter 5) and *So You Want to Start a House Church* (Chapter 2) for a discussion on the difference between the church and the work.

[7] Acts 20:20.

functioning. When Paul writes his letters to the churches in Corinth and Rome, he addresses the entire church (and not leaders) and asks the whole church to resolve its own problems.

They [the Jews in Rome] arranged to meet Paul on a certain day, and came in even larger numbers to the place where he was staying. From morning till evening he explained and declared to them the Kingdom of God and tried to convince them about Jesus from the Law of Moses and from the Prophets . . . Then he stayed two whole years in his own rented house. And he welcomed all who visited him, proclaiming the Kingdom of God and teaching the things concerning the Lord Jesus Christ with full boldness and without hindrance.

-Acts 28:23, 30-31

CHAPTER 7

THE KINGDOM COMES TO ROME
A.D. 59 - A.D. 62

Paul spends two years in jail in Caesarea. He is then sent to Rome to be tried by Caesar. Luke and Aristarchus escort Paul on the journey. The three men take a ship to Rome. On their way there, there is a massive shipwreck. But no one is harmed.

When Paul gets to Rome, he is placed under house arrest and is allowed to entertain visitors. Because Paul's custom is to preach the gospel to the "Jew first," he sends for the Jewish leaders in the city. The Jewish leaders visit Paul for a day, and he preaches the Kingdom of God to them the entire time.[1]

Tychicus visits Paul to comfort him. Epaphras (also called Epaphraditus) visits Paul in Rome to alert him about the crisis in Colosse. The church in Colosse is being ravaged by false teachers. They are teaching that union with God requires keeping the Law of Moses and will be evidenced by special mystical experiences.

Onesimus, Philemon's slave, runs away from home and steals some of Philemon's money. Epaphras finds him and takes him to Rome with him.

On his way to Rome, Epaphras stops at the church in Philippi where he is well received. While there, he observes some of the problems the church is facing. Some of the sisters

---

[1] Acts 28:23.

are fighting. The church is also being troubled by those from the circumcision party as well as from those who are teaching that liberty in Christ is license to sin.

The church in Philippi gives Epaphras a financial gift to bring to Paul. As Epaphras leaves Philippi for Rome, he becomes deathly ill. Word is sent to Philippi to pray for his health.

Epaphras and Onesimus finally make it to Rome where they visit Paul. Paul leads Onesimus to the Lord. Epaphras gives Paul a report on the condition of the churches in Colosse and Philippi.

In response, Paul writes three letters. One to Colosse which addresses the present crisis, one to Philemon which asks him to forgive and receive Onesimus, and one to all the churches in Asia Minor. The latter letter is called Ephesians. Tychicus delivers all three letters.

Colossians

OUTLINE:

Universal: Christ the Head of the Universe.
Chapter 1

Spiritual: Christ the Fullness of the Godhead
Chapter 2

Local: Christ the Head of the Church.
Chapters 3-4

KINGDOM QUOTES:

Col. 1:3:   We always thank God, the Father of OUR LORD JESUS CHRIST, when we pray for you,

Col. 1:12: Giving thanks to the Father, who has qualified you to share in the inheritance of the saints in THE KINGDOM OF LIGHT.

Col. 1:13: For He has rescued us from the dominion of darkness and brought us into THE KINGDOM OF THE SON HE LOVES.

Col. 1:16: FOR BY HIM ALL THINGS WERE CREATED: THINGS IN HEAVEN AND ON EARTH, VISIBLE AND INVISIBLE, WHETHER THRONES OR POWERS OR RULERS OR AUTHORITIES; ALL THINGS WERE CREATED BY HIM AND FOR HIM.

Col. 1:18: And HE IS THE HEAD OF THE BODY, THE CHURCH; He is the beginning and the firstborn from among the dead, so that IN EVERYTHING HE MIGHT HAVE THE SUPREMACY.

Col. 2:6: So then, just as you received CHRIST JESUS AS LORD, continue to live in Him.

Col. 2:10: And you have been given fullness in CHRIST, WHO IS THE HEAD OVER EVERY POWER AND AUTHORITY.

Col. 2:15: AND HAVING DISARMED THE POWERS AND AUTHORITIES, HE MADE A PUBLIC SPEC-TACLE OF THEM, TRIUMPHING OVER THEM BY THE CROSS.

Col. 3:17: And whatever you do, whether in word or deed, do it all in the name of THE LORD JESUS, giving thanks to God the Father through Him.

Col. 3:24: Since you know that you will receive an inheritance from the Lord as a reward. It is the LORD CHRIST you are serving.

Col. 4:11: Jesus, who is called Justus, also sends greetings. These are the only Jews among my fellow workers for THE KINGDOM OF GOD, and they have proved a comfort to me.

Philemon

OUTLINE:

The Approach: Thanksgiving.
Verses 1-7

The Argument: A Spiritual Relationship.
Verses 8-16

The Appeal: Forgive and Receive.
Verses 17-25

KINGDOM QUOTES:

Phm. 1:3: Grace to you and peace from God our Father and THE LORD JESUS CHRIST.

Phm. 1:5: Because I hear about your faith in THE LORD JESUS and your love for all the saints.

Phm. 1:25: The grace of THE LORD JESUS CHRIST be with your spirit.

Ephesians

OUTLINE:

Wealth: The Church Seated in Heavenly Places.
Chapters 1-3

Walk: The Church Walking in the Lord.
Chapter 4-5

Warfare: The Church Standing Against the Enemy.
Chapter 6

KINGDOM QUOTES:

Eph. 1:2: Grace and peace to you from God our Father and THE LORD JESUS CHRIST.

Eph. 1:3: Praise be to the God and Father of OUR LORD JESUS CHRIST, who has blessed us in the heavenly realms with every spiritual blessing in Christ.

Eph. 1:10: To be put into effect when the times will have reached their fulfillment TO BRING ALL THINGS IN HEAVEN AND ON EARTH TOGETHER UNDER ONE HEAD, EVEN CHRIST.

Eph. 1:15: Ever since I heard about your faith in THE LORD JESUS and your love for all the saints . . .

Eph. 1:17: I keep asking that the God of OUR LORD JESUS CHRIST, the glorious Father, may give you the Spirit of wisdom and revelation, so that you may know Him better.

Eph. 1:20-22: . . . He raised Him from the dead and seated Him at His right hand in the heavenly realms, FAR ABOVE ALL RULE AND AUTHORITY, POWER AND DOMINION, AND EVERY TITLE THAT CAN BE GIVEN, NOT ONLY IN THE PRESENT AGE BUT ALSO IN THE ONE TO COME. AND GOD PLACED ALL THINGS UNDER HIS FEET AND APPOINTED HIM TO BE HEAD OVER EVERYTHING FOR THE CHURCH.

Eph. 3:11: According to His eternal purpose which He accomplished in CHRIST JESUS OUR LORD.

Eph. 4:15: Instead, speaking the truth in love, we will in all things grow up into HIM WHO IS THE HEAD, THAT IS, CHRIST.

Eph. 5:5: For of this you can be sure: No immoral, impure or greedy person—such a man is an idolater—has any inheritance in THE KINGDOM OF CHRIST AND OF GOD.

Eph. 5:20: Always giving thanks to God the Father for everything, in the name of OUR LORD JESUS CHRIST.

Eph. 5:23: For the husband is the head of the wife as CHRIST IS THE HEAD OF THE CHURCH, His body, of which He is the Savior.

Eph. 6:23: Peace to the brothers, and love with faith from God the Father and THE LORD JESUS CHRIST.

Eph. 6:24: Grace to all who love OUR LORD JESUS CHRIST with an undying love.

Philippi sends Paul a letter asking about Epaphras' health. Paul writes a letter to the church in Philippi to thank them for their financial gift, to give an update on Epaphras, and to address the problems the church is encountering.

Philippians

OUTLINE:

Experience: The Joy of the Lord.
Chapter 1:1-26

Exposition: The Mind of Christ.
Chapters 1:27-4:1

Exhortation: Resolving Problems.
Chapter 4:2-23

KINGDOM QUOTES:

Php. 1:2: Grace and peace to you from God our Father and THE LORD JESUS CHRIST.

Php. 2:11: . . . and every tongue confess that JESUS CHRIST IS LORD, to the glory of God the Father.

Php. 2:19: I hope in THE LORD JESUS to send Timothy to you soon, that I also may be cheered when I receive news about you.

Php. 3:8: What is more, I consider everything a loss compared to the surpassing greatness of knowing CHRIST JESUS MY LORD, for whose sake I have lost all things. I consider them rubbish, that I may gain Christ.

Php. 3:20: BUT OUR CITIZENSHIP IS IN HEAVEN. And we eagerly await a Savior from there, THE LORD JESUS CHRIST.

Php. 4:23: The grace of THE LORD JESUS CHRIST be with your spirit. Amen.

Paul spends two years under house arrest in Rome where he continues to teach and preach the Kingdom of God to all who visit him. Priscilla and Aquila move back to Ephesus.[2]

---

[2] This chapter is a summary of Acts 23:35-Acts 28:31, Colossians, Philemon, Ephesians, and Philippians.

OBSERVATIONS

The churches in Colosse, Ephesus, Philippi and Rome are enjoying and expressing the Kingdom of God. None of the churches have a shepherd or pastor but Jesus Christ, the King of kings and Lord of lords. Philippi and Ephesus have elders (overseers), but no pastor.

When Paul writes his letters to the churches in Colosse, Asia Minor (Ephesians), and Philippi, he appeals to all the believers and beseeches them to address their own problems.

The churches do not meet in religious buildings. The church in Ephesus meets in the home of Priscilla and Aquila as well as in other homes throughout the city.[3] The church in Colosse meets in the home of Philemon.[4] The church in Laodicea meets in the home of Nympha.[5]

---

[3] 1 Cor. 16:19; Acts 20:20.
[4] Phm. 1:2.
[5] Col. 4:15.

The seventh angel sounded his trumpet, and there were loud voices in heaven, which said: "The kingdom of the world has become the Kingdom of our Lord and of His Christ, and He will reign for ever and ever."

-Revelation 11:15

CHAPTER 8

THE KINGDOM COMES TO PATMOS
A.D. 63 - A.D. 70

After two years of being under house arrest in Rome, Paul is released. He travels to Spain and then to Crete to meet Titus. (Titus has planted a number of churches on the Island of Crete.)

Paul leaves Titus in Crete and heads to Asia Minor. Timothy is in Ephesus and sends word to Paul that the Ephesian church is being ravaged by false teachers. The teachers are promoting the following heresies: It is a sin to eat meat and engage in marriage; Eve was both a mediator and redeemer who pre-existed Adam; men and women are no longer subject to earthly authorities. The heresy finds fertile ground among some of the women in the church who promote it in the church meetings.

Paul visits Timothy in Ephesus to deal with the crisis. He then leaves for Macedonia. The crisis in Ephesus worsens, and Timothy writes to Paul about it. From Macedonia, Paul writes a letter to Timothy instructing him on how to deal with the false teaching.

1 Timothy

OUTLINE:

Charge to the Church: Her Functions.
Chapters 1-3

Charge to the Worker: His Duties.
Chapters 4-6

KINGDOM QUOTES:

1 Tim. 1:2: To Timothy my true son in the faith: Grace, mercy and peace from God the Father and CHRIST JESUS OUR LORD.

1 Tim. 1:12: I thank CHRIST JESUS OUR LORD, who has given me strength, that He considered me faithful, appointing me to His service.

1 Tim. 1:17: Now to THE KING eternal, immortal, invisible, the only God, be honor and glory for ever and ever. Amen.

1 Tim. 6:3: If anyone teaches false doctrines and does not agree to the sound instruction of OUR LORD JESUS CHRIST and to godly teaching . . .

1 Tim. 6:14: To keep this command without spot or blame until the appearing of OUR LORD JESUS CHRIST.

1 Tim. 6:15: . . . God, the blessed and ONLY RULER, THE KING OF KINGS AND LORD OF LORDS.

1 Tim. 6:19: In this way they will lay up treasure for themselves as a firm foundation FOR THE COMING AGE, so that they may take hold of the life that is truly life.

The Kingdom of God has spread throughout the Roman Empire. And the kingdom of darkness is gaining strength in its attempt to suppress it. Emperor Nero begins to violently persecute the Christians. The persecution moves throughout all of the Roman Empire.

The church in Rome comes under severe attack. As a result, some of the Hebrew believers in the church are digressing back to their Jewish traditions in order to circumvent the persecution. (Judaism is covered under Roman Law while Christianity is not.)

Apollos (or Barnabas) writes to the Hebrew Christians in Rome, encouraging them to continue to follow Christ and not turn back to the Law.[1]

---

[1] We do not know who wrote Hebrews, but Apollos, Barnabas, or Silas are the best candidates.

Hebrews

OUTLINE:

Argument: The Foundations for Faith.
Chapters 1:1-10:37

Appeal: The Fruitfulness of Faith.
Chapters 10:38-13:25

KINGDOM QUOTES:

Heb. 1:3: The Son is the radiance of God's glory and the exact representation of His being, sustaining all things by His powerful word. After He had provided purification for sins, HE SAT DOWN AT THE RIGHT HAND OF THE MAJESTY IN HEAVEN.

Heb. 1:8: But about the Son He says, "YOUR THRONE, O GOD, WILL LAST FOR EVER AND EVER, AND RIGHTEOUSNESS WILL BE THE SCEPTER OF YOUR KINGDOM . . ."

Heb. 2:5: It is not to angels that HE HAS SUBJECTED THE WORLD TO COME, about which we are speaking.

Heb. 6:5: Who have tasted the goodness of the word of God and THE POWERS OF THE COMING AGE.

Heb. 7:1-3: This Melchizedek was KING OF SALEM and priest of God Most High. He met Abraham returning from the defeat of the kings and blessed him, and Abraham gave him a tenth of everything. First, his name means "KING OF RIGHTEOUSNESS;" then also, "KING OF SALEM" means "KING OF PEACE." Without father or mother, without genealogy, without beginning of days or end of life, LIKE THE SON OF GOD he remains a priest forever.

Heb. 8:1: The point of what we are saying is this: We do have such a high priest, WHO SAT DOWN AT THE RIGHT HAND OF THE THRONE OF THE MAJESTY IN HEAVEN.

Heb. 12:28: Therefore, since we are receiving A KINGDOM THAT CANNOT BE SHAKEN, let us be thankful, and so worship God acceptably with reverence and awe.

Heb. 13:20: May the God of peace, who through the blood of the eternal covenant brought back from the dead OUR LORD JESUS, that great Shepherd of the sheep . .

Paul gets word from Titus that the churches on the Island of Crete are still in crisis. The men in the church are being influenced by the self-indulgent Cretan lifestyle. There is rebellion against local authorities, and some of the women are slandering others and abusing alcohol. Paul writes Titus and instructs him on how to handle the crisis.

Titus

OUTLINE:

Church Life: Authority.
Chapter 1

Church Activity: Behavior.
Chapter 2

Church Duty: Witness.
Chapter 3[2]

Paul winters in Nicopolis, Greece where he preaches the Kingdom and plants a church. Paul leaves for Ephesus. But on his way, he is taken captive by local authorities and imprisoned in Rome.

John, the apostle, moves to Ephesus. The churches in Asia Minor are being ravaged by false prophets who are teaching the following: The physical world is evil so Jesus could not have come in physical flesh; Jesus was not the Son of God; a person can sin all they want and it will not affect their spiritual life. John responds to the influence of the false prophets by writing three letters.

---

[2] There are no "Kingdom Quotes" for Titus.

1 John

OUTLINE:

Fellowship: God is Light.
Chapters 1-2

Walking: God is Love.
Chapters 3-4

Living: God is Life.
Chapter 5

2 John

OUTLINE:

Love: A Commandment.
Verses 1-5

Light: A Definition.
Verse 6

Life: A Warning.
Verses 7-13

3 John

OUTLINE:

Gaius: Love Practiced.
Verses 1-8

Diotrephes: Love Violated.
Verses 9-10

Demetrius: Love Expressed.
Verses 11-14[3]

The churches in northwest Asia are suffering massive persecution. Peter and Silas have been laboring in this region for years. Upon hearing about their suffering, Peter sends a letter to the churches in northwest Asia to encourage them.

1 Peter

OUTLINE:

Confidence: Suffering and Faith.
Chapters 1:1-2:1

Conduct: Suffering and Holiness.
Chapters 2:2-3:9

---

[3] There are no "Kingdom Quotes" for John's epistles.

Character: Suffering and Victory.
Chapters 3:10-5:7

Conflict: Suffering and Warfare.
Chapter 5:8-14

KINGDOM QUOTES:

1 Pet. 1:3: Praise be to the God and Father of OUR LORD JESUS CHRIST!

1 Pet. 2:9: But you are a chosen people, A ROYAL PRIESTHOOD, a holy nation, a people belonging to God, that you may declare the praises of Him who called you out of darkness into His wonderful light.

1 Pet. 3:15: But in your hearts set apart CHRIST AS LORD.

1 Pet. 3:22: [JESUS CHRIST] WHO HAS GONE INTO HEAVEN AND IS AT GOD'S RIGHT HAND—WITH ANGELS, AUTHORITIES AND POWERS IN SUBMISSION TO HIM.

Paul's time is drawing to a close. He knows that the Lord will soon take him. He writes his last letter to Timothy, which both encourages and warns his young apprentice regarding the coming apostasy (falling away from the faith).

2 Timothy

OUTLINE:

Personal: Responsibility in Gifts and Grace.
Chapters 1:1-2:13

Church Life: Responsibility in Ministry.
Chapters 2:14-3:13

Spiritual Reality: Responsibility in Testimony.
Chapters 3:14-4:22

KINGDOM QUOTES:

2 Tim. 1:2: To Timothy, my dear son: Grace, mercy and peace from God the Father and CHRIST JESUS OUR LORD.

2 Tim. 2:12: If we endure, WE WILL ALSO REIGN WITH HIM. If we disown Him, He will also disown us.

2 Tim. 4:1: In the presence of God and of Christ Jesus, who will judge the living and the dead, and in view of His appearing and HIS KINGDOM . . .

2 Tim. 4:18: The Lord will rescue me from every evil attack and will bring me safely to HIS HEAVENLY KINGDOM. To Him be glory for ever and ever. Amen.

Peter knows he has little time left as well. He writes one more letter to the churches in northwest Asia, warning them about the coming false teachers.

2 Peter

OUTLINE:

Perseverance: Faithfulness to the Vision.
Chapters 1-2

Perils: The Coming False Teachers.
Chapter 3

KINGDOM QUOTES:

2 Pet. 1:2: Grace and peace be yours in abundance through the knowledge of God and of JESUS OUR LORD.

2 Pet. 1:8: For if you possess these qualities in increasing measure, they will keep you from being ineffective and unproductive in your knowledge of OUR LORD JESUS CHRIST.

2 Pet. 1:11: And you will receive a rich welcome into THE ETERNAL KINGDOM OF OUR LORD AND SAVIOR JESUS CHRIST.

2 Pet. 1:14: Because I know that I will soon put it aside, as OUR LORD JESUS CHRIST has made clear to me.

2 Pet. 1:16: We did not follow cleverly invented stories when we told you about the power and coming of OUR LORD JESUS CHRIST, but we were eyewitnesses of HIS MAJESTY.

2 Pet. 2:1: But there were also false prophets among the people, just as there will be false teachers among you. They will secretly introduce destructive heresies, even denying THE SOVEREIGN LORD who bought them—bringing swift destruction on themselves.

2 Pet. 2:20: If they have escaped the corruption of the world by knowing OUR LORD AND SAVIOR JESUS CHRIST and are again entangled in it and overcome, they are worse off at the end than they were at the beginning.

2 Pet. 3:18 : But grow in the grace and knowledge of OUR LORD AND SAVIOR JESUS CHRIST. To Him be glory both now and forever! Amen.

Peter and Paul are martyred in Rome. The false teachers that Peter warned about have appeared. Jude, the half-brother of Jesus, writes a letter to encourage God's people to contend for the authentic gospel, which is now under attack.

Jude

OUTLINE:

The Danger: Exposing False Teachers.
Verses 1-16

The Duty: Responding to False Teachers.
Verses 17-25

KINGDOM QUOTES:

Jude 1:4: For certain men whose condemnation was written about long ago have secretly slipped in among you. They are godless men, who change the grace of our God into a license for immorality and deny JESUS CHRIST OUR ONLY SOVEREIGN AND LORD.

Jude 1:17: But, dear friends, remember what the apostles of OUR LORD JESUS CHRIST foretold.

Jude 1:21: Keep yourselves in God's love as you wait for the mercy of OUR LORD JESUS CHRIST to bring you to eternal life.

Jude 1:25: TO THE ONLY GOD OUR SAVIOR BE GLORY, MAJESTY, POWER AND AUTHORITY, THROUGH JESUS CHRIST OUR LORD, BEFORE ALL AGES, NOW AND FOREVERMORE! AMEN.

John is exiled to the Island of Patmos. Jesus Christ appears to John and gives him a breathtaking revelation of His soon coming Kingdom and its triumph over the kingdom of darkness. John writes this revelation in a book called "The Revelation of Jesus Christ."

Since the day of Pentecost, the Kingdom of God has been "already" but "not yet." In the book of Revelation, John sees the "not yet" of the Kingdom in a riveting vision.

The main theme of the book of Revelation is the Kingship of Jesus Christ. He will return to earth as King of kings and Lord of lords; He will set up His throne on earth; He will put down all authority; and He will reign forever and ever with His chosen ones.[4]

Revelation

OUTLINE:

Introduction: Jesus Christ, Lord of His Church.
Chapters 1-3

Message: Jesus Christ, King of His Kingdom.
Chapters 4-22

KINGDOM QUOTES:

Rev. 1:6: . . . and has made us to be A KINGDOM and priests to serve His God and Father—to Him be glory and power for ever and ever! Amen.

Rev. 1:9: I, John, your brother and companion in the suffering AND KINGDOM and patient endurance that are ours in Jesus, was on the Island of Patmos because of the word of God and the testimony of Jesus.

---

[4] This chapter is a summary of Hebrews, 1 Timothy, 2 Timothy, Titus, 1 Peter, 2 Peter, 1 John, 2 John, 3 John, Jude, and Revelation with additional information added from Romans.

Rev. 2:26-27: To him that overcomes and does my will to the end, I WILL GIVE AUTHORITY OVER THE NATIONS—"HE WILL RULE THEM WITH AN IRON SCEPTER; HE WILL DASH THEM TO PIECES LIKE POTTERY"—JUST AS I HAVE RECEIVED AUTHORITY FROM MY FATHER.

Rev. 5:5: Then one of the elders said to me, "Do not weep! See, THE LION OF THE TRIBE OF JUDAH, THE ROOT OF DAVID, HAS TRIUMPHED. He is able to open the scroll and its seven seals."

Rev. 5:10: You have made them to be A KINGDOM and priests to serve our God, and THEY WILL REIGN ON THE EARTH.

Rev. 6:10: They called out in a loud voice, "How long, SOVEREIGN LORD, holy and true, until you judge the inhabitants of the earth and avenge our blood?"

Rev. 11:4: These are the two olive trees and the two lampstands that stand before THE LORD OF THE EARTH.

Rev. 11:15: The seventh angel sounded his trumpet, and there were loud voices in heaven, which said: "THE KINGDOM OF THE WORLD HAS BECOME THE KINGDOM OF OUR LORD AND OF HIS CHRIST, AND HE WILL REIGN FOR EVER AND EVER."

Rev. 11:17: . . . We give thanks to you, LORD GOD ALMIGHTY, THE ONE WHO IS AND WHO WAS,

BECAUSE YOU HAVE TAKEN YOUR GREAT POWER AND HAVE BEGUN TO REIGN.

Rev. 12:5: She gave birth to a son, a male child, WHO WILL RULE ALL THE NATIONS WITH AN IRON SCEPTER.

Rev. 12:10: Then I heard a loud voice in heaven say: "Now have come the salvation and the power and THE KINGDOM OF OUR GOD, AND THE AUTHORITY OF HIS CHRIST . . .

Rev. 15:3: . . . and sang the song of Moses the servant of God and the song of the Lamb: "Great and marvelous are your deeds, Lord God Almighty. Just and true are your ways, KING OF THE AGES.

Rev. 17:14: They will make war against the Lamb, but the Lamb will overcome them because HE IS LORD OF LORDS AND KING OF KINGS—and with Him will be His called, chosen and faithful followers.

Rev. 19:6: Then I heard what sounded like a great multitude, like the roar of rushing waters and like loud peals of thunder, shouting: "Hallelujah! For OUR LORD GOD ALMIGHTY REIGNS."

Rev. 19:15: Out of His mouth comes a sharp sword with which to strike down the nations. "HE WILL RULE THEM WITH AN IRON SCEPTER."

Rev. 19:16: On His robe and on His thigh He has this name written: KING OF KINGS AND LORD OF LORDS.

Rev. 20:4: I saw thrones on which were seated those who had been given authority to judge. And I saw the souls of those who had been beheaded because of their testimony for Jesus and because of the word of God. They had not worshiped the beast or his image and had not received his mark on their foreheads or their hands. THEY CAME TO LIFE AND REIGNED WITH CHRIST A THOUSAND YEARS.

Rev. 20:6: Blessed and holy are those who have part in the first resurrection. The second death has no power over them, but THEY WILL BE PRIESTS OF GOD AND OF CHRIST AND WILL REIGN WITH HIM FOR A THOU-SAND YEARS.

Rev. 22:5: There will be no more night. They will not need the light of a lamp or the light of the sun, for the Lord God will give them light. AND THEY WILL REIGN FOR EVER AND EVER.

Rev. 22:20: He who testifies to these things says, "Yes, I am coming soon." Amen. Come, LORD JESUS.

Rev. 22:21: The grace of THE LORD JESUS be with God's people. Amen.

OBSERVATIONS

While undergoing massive persecution, the churches in Rome, Asia Minor, and northwest Asia are standing for the Kingdom of God. None of the churches have a shepherd or pastor but Jesus Christ, the King of kings and Lord of lords. None of the churches have a fixed liturgy. None of them have erected sacred buildings. While some of the churches have elders, the elders provide oversight only and not rulership, domination, or exclusive ministry.[5]

After the first century closes, the churches slowly begin to take a turn. They begin adopting man-made leadership structures that are part and parcel of the kingdoms of this world.[6] These leadership structures are contrary to the Kingdom of God, and they have been hindering its advancement since they were adopted by the Christian family. Consider our Lord's words:

> *. . . You know that the rulers of the Gentiles LORD IT OVER THEM, and their great men EXERCISE AUTHORITY OVER THEM. IT IS NOT SO AMONG YOU . . . (Matt. 20:25-26, NASB)*

> *. . . The kings of the Gentiles LORD IT OVER THEM; and those who HAVE AUTHORITY OVER THEM are called "Benefactors." BUT NOT SO WITH YOU . . . (Luke 22:25-26, NASB)*

---

[5] See my book *Who is Your Covering?* for a thorough discussion on the first-century role and function of elders and extra-local workers (apostles).

[6] For a comprehensive discussion on how and when these structures were introduced into the Christian faith, see my book *Pagan Christianity*.

In the final analysis, God will recover His church, and He will establish His Kingdom by it. Today, you and I are being summoned by the Lord to participate in this costly yet glorious restoration.

OUTLINE OF THE SCRIPTURES IN LIGHT OF THE KINGDOM OF GOD

The Old Testament		
Mediation and the Kingdom	The Priest	*Genesis to Deuteronomy*
Authority and the Kingdom	The Kings	*Joshua to Song of Songs*
Revelation and the Kingdom	The Prophets	*Isaiah to Malachi*

The New Testament		
The Mediator of the Kingdom	Christ as Priest	*Matthew to John*
The Authority of the Kingdom	Christ as King	*Acts*
The Revelation of the Kingdom	Christ as Prophet	*Romans to Revelation*

CHRONOLOGY OF
NEW TESTAMENT LITERATURE[7]

The Twenty-Seven Books of the New Testament

Book	Date	Written From	Written To
Galatians written by Paul	A.D. 49	Antioch, Syria	The four churches in South Galatia
James written by James	A.D. 50	Jerusalem	The dispersed Jewish Christians in Palestine
1 Thessalonians written by Paul	A.D. 51	Corinth	The church in Thessalonica
2 Thessalonians written by Paul	A.D. 52	Corinth	The church in Thessalonica
1 Corinthians written by Paul	A.D. 55	Ephesus	The church in Corinth
2 Corinthians written by Paul	A.D. 57	Macedonia	The church in Corinth
Romans written by Paul	A.D. 57	Corinth	The church in Rome
Mark written by Mark	late 50s-early 60s	Rome	Unknown

---

[7] See my book *The Untold Story of the New Testament Church* for details.

The Twenty-Seven Books of the New Testament

Matthew written by Matthew	late 50s-early 60s	Antioch, Syria	The Jews
Luke written by Luke	A.D. 60-61	Rome	Theophilus and the Gentiles
Colossians written by Paul	A.D. 61	Rome	The church in Colosse
Philemon written by Paul	A.D. 61	Rome	Philemon of Colosse
Ephesians written by Paul	A.D. 61	Rome	The churches in Asia Minor
Philippians written by Paul	A.D. 62	Rome	The church in Philippi
1 Timothy written by Paul	A.D. 63	Macedonia	Timothy in Ephesus
Acts written by Luke	A.D. 63	Macedonia	Theophilus and the Gentiles
Hebrews probably written by Apollos, Barnabas, or Silas	A.D. 64	Unknown	The Hellenistic Jewish believers in Rome
Titus written by Paul	A.D. 65	Macedonia	Titus in Crete
John written by John	A.D. 65	Ephesus	Unknown
1 John written by John	A.D. 65	Ephesus	The churches in Asia Minor

The Twenty-Seven Books of the New Testament

2 John written by John	A.D. 65	Ephesus	An unknown church in Asia Minor
3 John written by John	A.D. 65	Ephesus	Gaius in Asia Minor
1 Peter written by Peter	A.D. 65	Rome	The churches in northwest Asia
2 Timothy written by Paul	A.D. 67	Rome	Timothy in Ephesus
2 Peter written by Peter	A.D. 67	Rome	The churches in northwest Asia
Jude written by Jude	A.D. 68	Unknown	The dispersed Jewish Christians in and outside of Palestine
Revelation written by John	A.D. 70	Patmos	Seven churches in Asia Minor

THE PAULINE LETTERS

The Letters of Paul			
Galatians *1 Corinthians* *2 Corinthians* *Romans*	*1 Thessalonians* *2 Thessalonians*	*Ephesians* *Colossians* *Philemon* *Philippians*	*1 Timothy* *2 Timothy* *Titus*
The Kingdom and the Cross	The Kingdom to Come	The Kingdom and the Church	The Kingdom and the Work
Polemic	Prophetic	Philosophic	Pastoral
Faith	Hope	Love	Order
Controversial	Anticipative	Contemplative	Administrative
Plan of Salvation	Perfecting of Salvation	Privileges of Salvation	Purpose of Salvation
Soteriological	Eschatological	Christological	Ecclesiological

PAUL'S CHURCH PLANTING JOURNEYS[1]

Churches Planted by Paul			
1st Journey	*2nd Journey*	*3rd Journey*	*4th Journey*
A.D. 47-49	A.D. 50-52	A.D. 54-57	A.D. 63-65
Antioch (of Pisidia) Iconium Lystra Derbe	Philippi Thessalonica Berea Corinth	Ephesus Troas Illyricum Rome (transplanted)	Nicopolis Miletus

Chronology of Paul's Letters				
2nd Journey	*3rd Journey*	*Roman Jail 1*	*4th Journey*	*Roman Jail 2*
A.D. 50-52	A.D. 54-57	A.D. 60-62	A.D. 63-65	A.D. 65-67
Galatians[2] 1 Thess. 2 Thess.	1 Corinthians 2 Corinthians Romans	Colossians Philemon Ephesians Philippians	1 Timothy Titus	2 Timothy

---

[1] See my book *The Untold Story of the New Testament Church* for details.

[2] Paul actually wrote Galatians in A.D. 49 just before his second apostolic journey.

PAUL'S CAPTIVITY LETTERS

Paul's First Imprisonment Letters A.D. 60-62			
COLOSSIANS	*EPHESIANS*	*PHILIPPIANS*	*PHILEMON*
To a church	Circuit letter	To a church	To an individual
Christ the Head	Christ the Body	Christ the Servant	Christ the Forgiver
Christ is ALL	ALL in Christ	Christ in the Local Assembly	Christ in the Home
The Kingdom and the Cosmos	The Kingdom and the Churches	The Kingdom and the Community	The Kingdom and the Christian

THE NON-PAULINE LETTERS

The Letters of James, John, Peter, Jude, and Hebrews			
2 Peter *Jude* *Revelation*	*1 John* *2 John* *3 John*	*James* *1 Peter*	*Hebrews*
The Kingdom and the Last Days	The Kingdom and Eternal Life	The Kingdom and Christian Ethics	The Kingdom and the Priest- hood
Prophetic	Pastoral	Polemic	Philosophic
Hope	Life	Love	Faith
Christ as King	Christ as Life	Christ as Righteousness	Christ as High Priest
The Climax of Salvation	The Evidence of Salvation	The Conduct of Salvation	The Basis for Salvation
Eschatological	Spiritual	Ethical	Christological

BIBLIOGRAPHY

This informal bibliography makes no pretense at being exhaustive. It merely attempts to supply the reader with the source materials used in this book. Commonly debated subjects like the North Galatian vs. South Galatian hypothesis, the theory that Paul experienced an Ephesian imprisonment, and scholarly disputes over NT chronology, the date, provenance, and authorship of each NT book are treated in many of these volumes.

The Kingdom of God

Austin-Sparks, T. *The Ultimate Issue of the Universe,* Testimony Book Ministry.
Beasley-Murray, G.R. *Jesus and the Kingdom of God,* Eerdmans.
Bright, John. *The Kingdom of God,* Abingdon.
Cullmann, Oscar. *Christ and Time,* Westminster.
Dodd, C.H. *Parables of the Kingdom,* Scribner's.
Green, Joel. *Kingdom of God,* Bristol.
Jones, E. Stanley. *Is the Kingdom of God Realism?,* Abingdon-Cokesbury.
_____. *The Unshakable Kingdom and the Unchanging Person,* McNett Press.
Kraybill, Donald. *The Upside-Down Kingdom,* Herald Press.
Ladd, George. *A Theology of the New Testament,* Eerdmans.
_____. *Presence of the Future: The Eschatology of Biblical Realism,* Eerdmans.
_____. *Crucial Questions About the Kingdom of God,* Eerdmans.
_____. *The Gospel of the Kingdom: Popular Expositions on the Kingdom of God,* Paternoster Press.
Nee, Watchman. *Love Not the World,* Tyndale House.
Sauer, Eric. *The King of the Earth,* Paternoster Press.
Shenk, David and Ervin Stutzman. *Creating Communities of the Kingdom,* Herald Press.
Snyder, Howard. *A Kingdom Manifesto: Calling the Church to Live Under God's Reign,* InterVarsity Press.
_____. *Models of the Kingdom,* Wipf & Stock.
_____. *The Community of the King,* InterVarsity Press.
Vos, Geerhardus. *The Pauline Eschatology,* P & R Press.
Wimber, John. *Power Evangelism,* Harper & Row.
_____. *Power Healing,* HarperSanFrancisco.
Witherington, Ben. *The Realm of the Reign: Reflections on the Dominion of God,* Discipleship Resources.
Yoder, John Howard. *The Politics of Jesus,* Eerdmans.
Young, W.A. *What on Earth is the Kingdom of God?,* Xulon Press.

Paul's Life and Ministry

Ball, Charles Ferguson. *The Life and Times of the Apostle Paul*, Tyndale.

Bornkamm, Gunther. *Paul*, Harper and Row.

Bruce, F.F. *In the Steps of the Apostle Paul*, Kregel.

_____. *Jesus and Paul: Places They Knew,* Thomas Nelson.

_____. *Paul: Apostle of the Heart Set Free*, Eerdmans.

_____. *The Pauline Circle*, Paternoster Press.

Coneybeare W.J. and J.S. Howson. *The Life and Epistles of St. Paul*, Eerdmans.

Galli, Mark, ed. *Paul and His Times: Christian History Magazine*, Christianity Today Publishers.

Glover, T.R. *Paul of Tarsus*, Hendrickson.

Grant, Michael. *Paul in the Roman World: The Conflict at Corinth*, Westminister Press.

Hawthorne, Gerald F., Ralph P. Martin, Daniel G. Reid, eds. *Dictionary of Paul and His Letters,* InterVarsity Press.

Hengel, Martin. *Paul Between Damascus and Antioch: The Unknown Years,* John Knox Press.

Meinardus, Otto F.A. *St. Paul in Ephesus and the Cities of Galatia and Cyprus,* Lycabettus Press.

_____. *St. Paul in Greece,* Lycabettus Press.

_____. *St. Paul's Last Journey,* Melissa Media (or Caratzas Brothers Publishing).

_____. *St. John of Patmos and the Seven Churches of the Apocalypse,* Lycabettus Press.

Marshall, David. *Footprints of Paul*, Autumn House.

Murphy-O'Connor, Jerome. *Paul: A Critical Life*, Clarendon Press.

_____. *Paul the Letter-Writer: His World, His Options, His Skills*, The Liturgical Press.

Pollock, John. *The Man Who Shook the World*, Victor Books.

Porter, Stanley E. *Paul in Acts*, Hendrickson.

Rainer, Riesner. *Paul's Early Period: Chronology, Mission Strategy, Theology,* Eerdmans.

Ramsey, W.M. *St. Paul the Traveler and Roman Citizen*, Hodder and Stoughton.

Smith, David. *Life and Letters of St. Paul*, Harper Brothers.

White, Jefferson. *Evidence & Paul's Journeys*. Parsagard Press.

Winter, Bruce. *When Paul Left Corinth: The Influence of Secular Ethics and Social Change,* Eerdmans.

Witherington, Ben. *The Paul Quest: The Renewed Search for the Jew of Tarsus,* InterVarsity Press.

Worth, Roland H. *The Seven Cities of the Apocalypse and Greco-Asian Culture,* Paulist Press.

The Acts Narrative

Bruce, F.F. *The Acts of the Apostles: Greek Text with Introduction and Commentary,* Wipf & Stock.
_____. *The Book of the Acts (Revised, 1988 Edition),* Eerdmans.
Hemer, Colin J. *The Book of Acts in the Setting of Hellenistic History,* J.C.B. Mohr.
Guthrie, Donald. *The Apostles,* Zondervan.
Marshall, I. Howard. *The Acts of the Apostles,* InterVarsity Press.
Scroggie, W. Graham. *The Unfolding Drama of Redemption: Volume 2,* Kregel.
Wenham, David and Steve Walton. *Exploring the New Testament: A Guide to the Gospels and Acts,* Society for Promoting Christian Knowledge.
Winter, Bruce, ed. *The Book of Acts in Its First Century Setting (6 Volumes),* Eerdmans.
_____. Volume 1: *The Book of Acts in Its Ancient Literary Setting,* Eerdmans.
_____. Volume 2: *The Book of Acts in Its Graeco-Roman Setting,* Eerdmans.
_____. Volume 3: *The Book of Acts and Paul in Roman Custody,* Eerdmans.
_____. Volume 4: *The Book of Acts in Its Palestinian Setting,* Eerdmans.
_____. Volume 5: *The Book of Acts in Its Diaspora Setting,* Eerdmans.
_____. Volume 6: *The Book of Acts in Its Theological* Setting, Eerdmans.
Witherington, Ben. *History, Literature, and Society in the Book of Acts,* Cambridge University Press.
_____. *The Acts of the Apostles: A Socio-Rhetorical Commentary,* Eerdmans.

The New Testament Epistles

Bruce, F.F. *The Epistles of John,* Eerdmans.
Guthrie, Donald. *New Testament Introduction,* InterVarsity Press.
Marshall, I. Howard, Steven Travis, & Ian Paul. *Exploring the New Testament: A Guide to the Letters & Revelation,* InterVarsity Press.
New Century Bible (New Testament Series), Oliphants.
New International Biblical Commentary (New Testament Series), Hendrickson.
Roetzel, Calvin. *The Letters of Paul: Conversations in Context,* Westminster John Knox Press.
The New International Commentary of the New Testament, Eerdmans.
The New International Greek Testament Commentary, Eerdmans.
The Tyndale New Testament Commentaries, Inter-Varsity Press.
Witherington, Ben. *Grace in Galatia: A Commentary on Paul's Letter to the Galatians,* Eerdmans.
_____. *Conflict & Community in Corinth: A Socio-Rhetorical Commentary on 1 and 2 Corinthians,* Eerdmans.
_____. *Paul's Letter to the Romans: A Socio-Rhetorical Commentary,* Eerdmans.
_____. *Revelation,* The New Cambridge Bible Commentary.
Word Biblical Commentary (New Testament Portion), Word Books.

Life in the Roman Empire

Blaiklock, E.M. *Cities of the New Testament*, Fleming Revell.
Casson, Lionel. *Everyday Life in Ancient Rome*, John Hopkins University Press.
_____. *Travel in the Ancient World*, John Hopkins University Press.
Corbishley, Mike. *What Do We Know About the Romans?*, Peter Bedrick Books.
Cornell, Tim and John Matthews. *Atlas of the Roman World*, Facts on File, Inc.
Durant, Will. *Caesar and Christ*, Simon and Schuster.
Harris, William. *Ancient Literacy*, Harvard University Press.
Goodenough, Simon. *Citizens of Rome*, Crown Publishers.
King, Marie Gentert, Ed. *Foxe's Book of Martyrs*, Spire Books.
Lampe, Peter. *From Paul to Valentinus: Christians at Rome in the First Two Centuries*, Fortress.
Liversidge, Joan. *Everyday Life in the Roman Empire*, G.P. Putnam's Sons.
Macaulay, David. *City: A Story of Roman Planning and Construction*, Houghton Mifflin Co.
Marks, A.J. and G.I.F. Tingay. *The Romans*, EDC Publishing.
Ramsey, W.M. *The Church in the Roman Empire*, G.P. Putnam's Sons.
Rhoads, David M. *Israel in Revolution 6-74 C.E.*, Fortress Press.
Saller, Richard. *The Roman Empire: Economy, Society, and Culture*, Berkeley.
Smallwood, E. Mary. *The Jews Under Roman Rule*, Leiden.
Winter, Bruce. *Roman Wives, Roman Widows: The Appearance of New Women and the Pauline Communities*, Eerdmans.
_____. *Seeking the Welfare of the City: Christians as Benefactors and Citizens*, Eerdmans.

The Social, Cultural, and Political Background of the New Testament Church

Barr, David. *An Introduction: New Testament Story*, Wadsworth Publishing Company.
Bruce, F.F. *New Testament History*, Doubleday.
_____. *Peter, Stephen, James & John: Studies in Non-Pauline Christianity*, Eerdmans.
Evans, Craig and Stanley Porter, eds. *Dictionary of New Testament Background*, InterVarsity Press.
Ferguson, Everett. *Backgrounds of Early Christianity*, Eerdmans.
Jeffers, James. *The Greco-Roman World of the New Testament Era: Exploring the Background of Early Christianity*, InterVarsity Press.
Judge, E. A. *The Social Pattern of Christian Groups in the First Century*, Tyndale Press.
Malherbe, Abraham J. *Social Aspects of Early Christianity*, Fortress Press.
Martin, Ralph P. and Peter Davids, eds. *Dictionary of the Later New Testament & Its Development*, InterVarsity Press.
Meeks, Wayne. *The First Urban Christians: The Social World of the Apostle Paul*, Yale University Press.
_____. *The Moral World of the First Christians*, John Knox Press.

Miller, Wayne D. *New Testament Churches*, Miller Publications.
Stambaugh, John E. and David L. Balch. *The New Testament in Its Social Environment*, The Westminster Press.
Stark, Rodney. *The Rise of Christianity: A Sociologist Reconsiders History*, Princeton University Press.
Stowers, Stanley. *Letter Writing in Greco-Roman Antiquity*, John Knox Press.
Theissen, Gerd. *Social Reality and the Early Christians: Theology, Ethics, and the World of the New Testament*, Fortress Press.
Tidball, Derek. *The Social Context of the New Testament: Sociological Analysis*, Zondervan.
Witherington, Ben. *New Testament History: A Narrative Account*, Baker Books.

The Chronology of the First-Century Church

Barker, Kenneth, ed. "Timeline of Paul's Life," *The NIV Study Bible*, Zondervan.
Bruce, F.F. *Chronological Questions in the Acts of the Apostles*, J. Rylands.
Finegan, Jack. *Handbook of Biblical Chronology*, Princeton University Press.
Gunther, John J. *Paul: Messenger and Exile: A Study in the Chronology of His Life and Letters*, Judson Press.
Hoehner, Harold. "A Chronological Table of the Apostolic Age," *Chronological and Background Charts to the New Testament*, ed. H. Wayne House, Zondervan.
_____. *Chronological Aspects of the Life of Christ*, Zondervan.
_____. "New Testament Chronology," *Nelson's Illustrated Bible Dictionary*, Nelson.
Jewett, Robert. *A Chronology of Paul's Life*, Fortress Press.
Ludemann, Gerd. *Paul, Apostle to the Gentiles: Studies in Chronology*, Fortress.
Ogg, George. *The Chronology of the Life of Paul*, Epworth.
_____. "Chronology of the New Testament," *New Bible Dictionary (Second Edition)*, InterVarsity Press.
Piper, John. "New Testament Chronology," *Encyclopedia of the Bible*, Baker.
Robinson, John A.T. *Redating the New Testament*, The Westminster Press.

Chronological and/or Dated Bibles

Acts in First-Person by the Men Who Lived It, SeedSowers.
Berkeley Version of the New Testament by Gerrit Verkuyl, Zondervan.
The Greatest Story by Johnston Cheney, Multnomah.
The Letters of Paul: An Expanded Paraphrase by F.F. Bruce, Eerdmans.
The Narrated Bible in Chronological Order by F. LaGard Smith, Harvest House.
The New Testament: A Translation by William Barclay, Westminster/John Knox Press.
The Seamless Bible by Charles Roller, Destiny Image.
The Story of My Life as Told by Jesus Christ, SeedSowers.

OTHER BOOKS BY FRANK VIOLA

Series on Radical Church Reform

Volume 1: Rethinking the Wineskin: The Practice of the New Testament Church. This is Frank Viola's classic book on the first-century church. It demonstrates beyond dispute that the modern institutional church has no Scriptural right to exist!

Volume 2: Who is Your Covering? A Fresh Look at Leadership, Authority, and Accountability. This book explores the issues of church leadership and spiritual authority in much more depth than *Wineskin.*

Volume 3: Pagan Christianity: The Origins of Our Modern Church Practices. A unique work that traces every modern Protestant practice, proving that it has no root in the NT.

Volume 4: So You Want to Start a House Church? First-Century Styled Church Planting. A must read after completing *Rethinking the Wineskin.* This book discusses the apostolic pattern for planting NT-styled churches. It also answers the question: "What shall I do now that I have left the organized church?"

Other Books

The Untold Story of the New Testament Church: An Extraordinary Guide to Understanding the New Testament. A detailed re-telling of the entire story of the first-century church in chronological order. This book gives the entire background to each letter in the NT.

Knowing Christ Together. A unique and insightful discussion on walking with the Lord with other believers.

Straight Talk to Elders. A thorough and compelling survey from Matthew to Revelation on the role and function of first-century elders and pastors.

For these titles and more, visit our ever-growing web site: **www.ptmin.org**

To obtain further information about first-century styled church life, email us at **PTMIN@aol.com**